MONSTER ACROSTICS

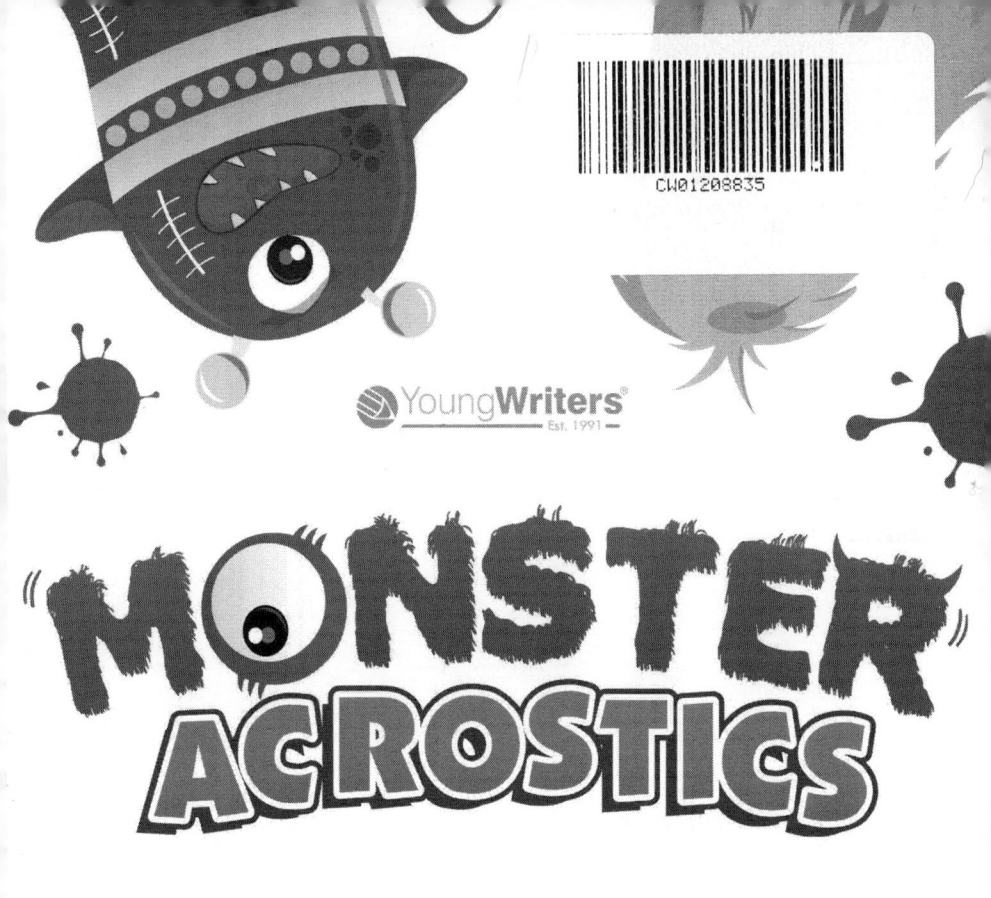

Under The Bed

Edited By Andy Porter

First published in Great Britain in 2024 by:

YoungWriters® Est. 1991

Young Writers
Remus House
Coltsfoot Drive
Peterborough
PE2 9BF
Telephone: 01733 890066
Website: www.youngwriters.co.uk

All Rights Reserved
Book Design by Ashley Janson
© Copyright Contributors 2024
Softback ISBN 978-1-83565-754-6
Printed and bound in the UK by BookPrintingUK
Website: www.bookprintinguk.com
YB0605W

Foreword

Welcome Reader,

For Young Writers' latest competition Monster Acrostics, we asked primary school pupils to create a monster then write an acrostic poem about it. The acrostic is a fantastic introduction to poetry writing as it comes with a built-in structure, allowing children to focus on their creativity and vocabulary choice.

We live and breathe creativity here at Young Writers and we want to pass our love of the written word onto the next generation – what better way to do that than to celebrate their writing by publishing it in a book!

Featuring all kinds of crazy creatures, strange beasts and mythical monsters, this anthology is brimming with imagination and creativity, showcasing the blossoming writing skills of these young poets. They have brought their creations to life using the power of words, resulting in some brilliant and fun acrostic poems!

Each awesome little poet in this book should be super proud of themselves! We hope you will delight in these poems as much as we have.

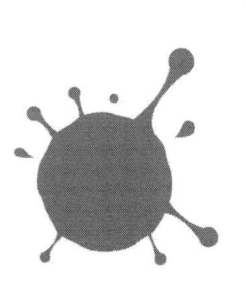

Contents

Ancrum Road Primary School, Dundee

Alana Calder (8)	1
Jake Macdonald (8)	2
Charlie Gardiner (8)	3
Jack Devine (8)	4
Erin Phillips (7)	5
George Robertson (7)	6
Rana Almutairi (8)	7
Shelby Black (7)	8
Avery McGrath (7)	9

Lakeside Primary School, Cheltenham

Yasmin Cook (5)	10
Rosalie Clarke (5)	11
Charlie Smith (6)	12
Sebby Wright (6)	13
Prishafa Laraddin Galatri (5)	14

Lockwood Primary School, Saltburn-by-the-Sea

Cooper Knight (6)	15
Jimmy Corner (5)	16
Luca Raw (6)	17
Alahna-Rose Foggin (6)	18
Harley Porritt (6)	19
Josie Rymer (6)	20
Harriet Smith (6)	21
Skylar Bennison (5)	22
Robbie Thornton (6)	23
Olivia Robshaw (6)	24
Sofia Crawford (5)	25

Freddie Mitchell (5)	26
Harper Henderson (6)	27
Bobby Gent (6)	28
Archie Elders (6)	29
Patrick Waterson (6)	30
Lottie Johnson (6)	31
Harrison Crellin (6)	32
Heidi Richardson (6)	33
Esmay Wiles (5)	34
George Robinson (5)	35

Matlock Bath Holy Trinity CE Controlled Primary School, Matlock Bath

Rosalinda Brailsford (6)	36
Charlie Watson (5)	37
Paige Winter (5)	38
Florence Burton (6)	39

Morland Primary School, Ipswich

Jaxon Starkie (6)	40
Rhea Gray (6)	41
Teddy Woods (7)	42
James Davies (7)	43
Amelia Bardwell (7)	44
Moana Theobald (6)	45
Ava Pike (7)	46
Brody Allan (7)	47
Layla Dunn (7)	48
Logan Mannering (6)	49
Paisleigh King (7)	50
Jaxon Allaton (6)	51
Marcello Moore (7)	52
Harry Upson (6)	53

Angelica Porter (7)	54
Skyla Clark (6)	55
Lucia Jordan (7)	56
Zamar Oduro Bonsu (7)	57
Abigail Javier (7)	58
Freyah Baker (6)	59
Santhosh Ramkumar (7)	60
Leo Marshall (7)	61
Ashlee Kerry (6)	62
Max Hill (6)	63
Amila Notkute (6)	64
Joey Bantoft (7)	65
Harley Carden (7)	66
Kasia Borowicka (7)	67
Sam Tunner (7)	68
Logan Pennock (4)	69
Rogan Sesto (5)	70
Harry Norman (5)	71
Cavalli-Lee Waight (4)	72
Dulcie Rouse (5)	73
Lola Wintrup (6)	74
Jax Pretlove (6)	75
Scarlett Lewis (4)	76
Riley Davis (5)	77
Rosie Minns (5)	78
Sienna Worby (4)	79
Maxwell Ologunja (5)	80
Sienna Bantoft (4)	81
Conor Mortimer (5)	82
Ovidas Cizas (5)	83
Scarlett Chapman (5)	84
Tabitha Robinson Kathirchelvan (5)	85
Kayden Kalyia (5)	86
Kinsley Broadhurst (5)	87
Archie Pike (4)	88
Mya Broadhurst (6)	89
Marley Wells (5)	90
Sofia Theobald (4)	91
Peyton Garner (5)	92
Edena Brazlauskaite (5)	93
Amelia Baker (5)	94
Luna Usman (6)	95
Olivia Garwood (4)	96
Arthur Davies (5)	97
Riley Richmond (5)	98
Remy Hunt (5)	99
Hunter Drury (5)	100
Oliver Baldry (6)	101
Leo Kelly (6)	102
Piper Simpson (6)	103
Hazel Garnham (6)	104
Karson Thompson (6)	105
Arthur Heasman (6)	106
Oscar Holder (6)	107

New Silksworth Academy, New Silksworth

Mirabel Anyanwu (6)	108
Alana Mullins (6)	109
Reuben Frame (6)	110
Scarlett Bird (6)	111
Michelle Anyanwu (6)	112
Louisa Davidson (5)	113
CharlieAnn Docherty (6)	114

St Philip's CE Primary School, Salford

Bailey Jones (7)	115
Cheryl Chick (7)	116
Aydin Tumusime (6)	117
George Burton (7)	118
Liam Nduonofit (7)	119
Albie Thorpe (7)	120
Elaine Ibrahim (6)	121
Jimmi Cheung (7)	122
Sean Tsang (7)	123
Hollie Wraight (7)	124
Christopher Kwok (6)	125
Victoria Lyu (6)	126
Harriett Paisley (7)	127
Leena Tijani (7)	128
Othman Aljasim (8)	129

Ysgol Bryn Garth Primary School, Penyffordd

Izabella Sharp (7)	130
Natalie Talay-Lopez (6)	131
Lewis Lacey (7)	132
Ivy Johns (6)	133
Willow Peyton (7)	134
Hallie Jones (7)	135
Heidi Jones (6)	136
Lottie Tellett Danks (7)	137
Louie Farbrace-Bellis (7)	138
Esme Roberts (7)	139
Niamh Power (5)	140
Margo Johns (6)	141
Charlie Palmer (5)	142
Zed Galing (6)	143
Eliza Lavelle (5)	144
Layla Lister (6)	145
Faith Jones (7)	146

The Poems

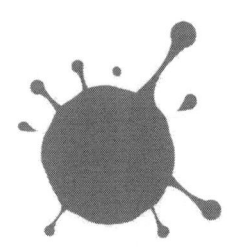

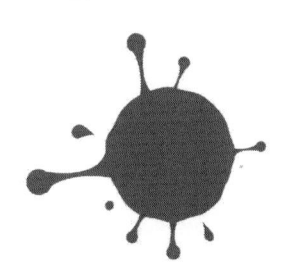

Threeyes

T hree big eyes
H ands are so soft and fluffy
R eally scary, lurks in the night
E ager to play with children's yo-yos
E ggs are her favourite food
Y ou should stay away!
E vil eyes and deathly stare
S alivating in the morning, sleeping at night.

Alana Calder (8)
Ancrum Road Primary School, Dundee

Monster

M y monster is mean, lazy and evil.
O ne big purple and green eye.
N eeds pink wings to fly.
S tinky when he eats really cold drinks.
T errifying in the dark night but good in the morning.
E yes as bright as the yellow sun.
R eally long, colourful legs.

Jake Macdonald (8)
Ancrum Road Primary School, Dundee

Blue Boots

B lue and beautiful wigs.
L uxurious and expensive bag.
U gly hair.
E ats like a beast.

B eautiful and long nails.
O ften bad.
O nly once a week she gets sweets.
T he tongue is pink.
S limy hair.

Charlie Gardiner (8)
Ancrum Road Primary School, Dundee

Rockets

R eally scary but stupid brains
O ne powerful, sparkly gem in the middle
C roaky voice scares the kind children
K arate chops his enemies
E xcellent eyesight and tough skin
T errorises everything
S limy and burnt skin.

Jack Devine (8)
Ancrum Road Primary School, Dundee

Terresa

T ough, big and brave.
E yes are very big and round.
R uns really badly and slowly.
R ude and ungrateful.
E ats small green bugs.
S leepy all of the time.
A lways throwing a tantrum and being naughty.

Erin Phillips (7)
Ancrum Road Primary School, Dundee

Scully

S cared by big, mean adults.
C old and yellow body.
U gly old thing and nice in the morning.
L ives in brown, hard boxes.
L oves to play with three to ten-year-olds.
Y ucky, hairy, slimy creature.

George Robertson (7)
Ancrum Road Primary School, Dundee

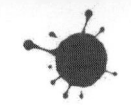

Monster Cate

M y monster is stinky.
O nly they are pink and blue and yellow.
N aughty and not nice.
S cary and always angry.
T ries to be that scary.
E ats a lot of food.
R eally has big eyes.

Rana Almutairi (8)
Ancrum Road Primary School, Dundee

Monster

M onsters who can fly.
O nly blue eyes.
N ever walking on six green legs.
S cary, yellow wings.
T errifying black horns.
E erie pink tongue.
R eally scary and grey.

Shelby Black (7)
Ancrum Road Primary School, Dundee

Peter G

P lays on Planet PK.
E nter the planet in three, two, one...
T he thighs are white.
E ars are invisible.
R ed and blue hands.

G iant teeth.

Avery McGrath (7)
Ancrum Road Primary School, Dundee

Slobadoba

S lobadoba has super sharp horns.
L oves to eat slime, bugs and bogeys.
O ne big, gooey eye.
B ig thumbs on his hands.
A very long tongue.
D eadly, sharp teeth.
O range, fluffy fur.
B lack, pointy ears.
A terrible roar.

Yasmin Cook (5)
Lakeside Primary School, Cheltenham

Silly Squid

S illy Squid the monster
I s always happy
L oves to eat goop
L ives on the moon
Y ellow, green and orange.

S limy and hairy
Q uick to move
U nder the stars
I n outer space
D oing the Silly Squid dance.

Rosalie Clarke (5)
Lakeside Primary School, Cheltenham

Fluffy

F luffy the monster
L ikes to catch people
U ses his fluffy arms
F un with his monster friends
F urry cuddles
Y ellow monster.

Charlie Smith (6)
Lakeside Primary School, Cheltenham

Slimy

S limy likes to eat bogeys.
L ucky Slimy because he is cool.
I like Slimy the best.
M y friend is Slimy.
Y ou can be friends with us.

Sebby Wright (6)
Lakeside Primary School, Cheltenham

Lilly

L illy the beautiful monster
I like her
L ikes to smile
L ikes pink and white
Y es, she is lovely.

Prishafa Laraddin Galatri (5)
Lakeside Primary School, Cheltenham

Terrible

T ough monster.
E ats strawberries.
R ed horns.
R eally scary.
I t is long.
B lue eyes.
L oves scaring people.
E ars are sharp.

Cooper Knight (6)
Lockwood Primary School, Saltburn-by-the-Sea

Naughty

N aughty monster.
A ngry at everyone.
U gly body.
G rabs people.
H orns are steaming red hot.
T ries to eat people.
Y ummy!

Jimmy Corner (5)
Lockwood Primary School, Saltburn-by-the-Sea

Steamy

S melly monster
T usks are sharp
E yes are googly
A mazing talent
M outh is wet
Y ucky arms.

Luca Raw (6)
Lockwood Primary School, Saltburn-by-the-Sea

Silly

S illy and sweet.
I nteresting, googly eyes.
L oves to play.
L ikes to be sneaky.
Y ellow crown.

Alahna-Rose Foggin (6)
Lockwood Primary School, Saltburn-by-the-Sea

Harley

H orrible.
A cts naughty.
R ed eyes.
L ives in a cave.
E ars are grey.
Y ellow body.

Harley Porritt (6)
Lockwood Primary School, Saltburn-by-the-Sea

Blump

B ig and beautiful.
L oves purple.
U nder control of itself.
M ad and mean.
P erfectly pink.

Josie Rymer (6)
Lockwood Primary School, Saltburn-by-the-Sea

Blump

B ig as a blimp
L oud as a lion
U gly as a blobfish
M ad as a hatter
P urple as a grape.

Harriet Smith (6)
Lockwood Primary School, Saltburn-by-the-Sea

Clive

C areful monster.
L ikes to play.
I t is orange.
V isits its friends.
E ats slimy bugs.

Skylar Bennison (5)
Lockwood Primary School, Saltburn-by-the-Sea

Arnie

A cts good
R ed, steaming horns
N aughty and scary
I ncredible monster
E normous ears.

Robbie Thornton (6)
Lockwood Primary School, Saltburn-by-the-Sea

Layla

L oves slime
A cts healthy
Y ellow, fluffy fur
L ives in a big house
A lways playing.

Olivia Robshaw (6)
Lockwood Primary School, Saltburn-by-the-Sea

Spots

S potty monster
P layful and kind
O range spots
T ries to be sneaky!
S leeps a lot.

Sofia Crawford (5)
Lockwood Primary School, Saltburn-by-the-Sea

Sniff

S limy green
N aughty monster
I ncredible, long legs
F luffy fur
F riendly monster.

Freddie Mitchell (5)
Lockwood Primary School, Saltburn-by-the-Sea

Blump

B lue skin.
L ikes to play.
U gly and mean.
M onster mouth.
P layful and nice.

Harper Henderson (6)
Lockwood Primary School, Saltburn-by-the-Sea

Swamp

S mall monster
W ears shiny boots
A ngry eyes
M ulticoloured
P ointy horns.

Bobby Gent (6)
Lockwood Primary School, Saltburn-by-the-Sea

Blake

B lue fur.
L ong legs.
A cts crazy.
K ind and beautiful.
E ats vegetables.

Archie Elders (6)
Lockwood Primary School, Saltburn-by-the-Sea

Scary

- **S** limy monster
- **C** lever
- **A** ngry with everyone
- **R** eally scary
- **Y** ucky teeth.

Patrick Waterson (6)
Lockwood Primary School, Saltburn-by-the-Sea

Blump

B lue skin
L oves to play
U gly and mean
M akes me happy
P lays games.

Lottie Johnson (6)
Lockwood Primary School, Saltburn-by-the-Sea

Sniff

S limy monster
N aughty
I s greedy
F angs are sharp
F inds a box.

Harrison Crellin (6)
Lockwood Primary School, Saltburn-by-the-Sea

Blob

B eautiful and small
L oves to play
O ne eye
B ouncing on a chair.

Heidi Richardson (6)
Lockwood Primary School, Saltburn-by-the-Sea

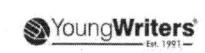

Blob

B ig and beautiful
L oves to eat
O ne eye
B ouncing all about.

Esmay Wiles (5)
Lockwood Primary School, Saltburn-by-the-Sea

Kind

K icks footballs
I s nice
N eeds fruit
D rinks water.

George Robinson (5)
Lockwood Primary School, Saltburn-by-the-Sea

Shally

S he is thoughtful.
H er heart is full of compassion.
A good friend.
L oves to be kind.
L ikes to help others.
Y ellow is her favourite colour.

Rosalinda Brailsford (6)
Matlock Bath Holy Trinity CE Controlled Primary School, Matlock Bath

Winger

W inger has super vision
I nvisible at night
N ever loses a fight
G iant as a house
E njoys playing with Endermen
R eally big wings.

Charlie Watson (5)
Matlock Bath Holy Trinity CE Controlled Primary School, Matlock Bath

Monsty

M onster is scary
O nly likes monsters
N early six years old
S limy and wet
T otally powerful
Y ellow-green skin.

Paige Winter (5)
Matlock Bath Holy Trinity CE Controlled Primary School, Matlock Bath

My Monster

S trange and cool.
I ncredible and important.
L onely and a bit rude.
L oving to me.
Y oung and fancy.

Florence Burton (6)
Matlock Bath Holy Trinity CE Controlled Primary School, Matlock Bath

Monster

M y monster is mysterious.
O nce ate a bug which didn't taste good.
N ibbles his food when he's not hungry.
S illy monster.
T wenty eyes to keep an eye out.
E ats ladybirds which are his favourite.
R eally slimy which means he leaves a trail behind him.

Jaxon Starkie (6)
Morland Primary School, Ipswich

Monster

M y monster is big and brave
O ften my monster sleeps all day
N asty my monster is and scary
S leeps, my monster does
T ickles, my monster does to people
E xtra excited to eat rotten eggs
R uns all around till dinnertime.

Rhea Gray (6)
Morland Primary School, Ipswich

Monster

M y monster is spooky and naughty
O ften eats little children
N aughty when he eats all of the food
S tomps and scares people away
T umbles down the hill
E ats little animals and little birds
R oars and wakes people up.

Teddy Woods (7)
Morland Primary School, Ipswich

Monster

M y monster has brown hair.
O n my monster, there is a lolly on top of it.
N o monster has slime on it.
S o stinky that it will smell up the room.
T wo monsters have teeth.
E very day they eat lollies.
R oar at people.

James Davies (7)
Morland Primary School, Ipswich

Monster

M oves really, really fast.
O ften swims in sticky, slimy pools.
N ibbles on adults' fingernails.
S harp horns to protect him.
T ickles people with his long nail.
E ats tall tree trunks.
R eally, really scary.

Amelia Bardwell (7)
Morland Primary School, Ipswich

Charlotte

C razy monster.
H appy, big monster.
A nnoying.
R eally wriggly monster.
L ong arms.
O nly scary.
T erribly terrifying face.
T all monster.
E xciting, huge monster.

Moana Theobald (6)
Morland Primary School, Ipswich

Monster

M ean and evil
O nly eats X-rays
N eeds to suck out eyeballs
S leeps during the day
T ough and trouble
E xtra six eyeballs
R ich and a criminal because he takes children's toys.

Ava Pike (7)
Morland Primary School, Ipswich

Monster

M akes sticky, gooey slime
O range, spiky horns
N ibbles children's smelly toes
S cary, small eye
T eeth are super sharp
E ats rubbish and mice tails
R uns super-duper fast.

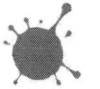

Brody Allan (7)
Morland Primary School, Ipswich

Monster

M akes lasers in his hands
O nly eats yellow medicine
N aughty and scary
S ticks to walls with his slimy skin
T ough and friendly
E ats children's toes
R uns super quick.

Layla Dunn (7)
Morland Primary School, Ipswich

Monster

M y monster is silly.
O ften really smelly.
N ever got makeup on.
S he's got orange hair.
T heir eyes are googly.
E yes are orange.
R *oar!* She likes to roar.

Logan Mannering (6)
Morland Primary School, Ipswich

Monster

M y monster lives under beds
O n a sunny day, she plays
N aughty to people she eats
S ix legs and she is really fast
T ummy is always rumbling
E ight arms
R uns all day.

Paisleigh King (7)
Morland Primary School, Ipswich

Fastdnyboilc

F unny
A nnoying
S cary
T all
D aydreams
N ice
Y ellow
B ad
O bvious
I t smells bad, claws
L ong, sharp
C hicken.

Jaxon Allaton (6)
Morland Primary School, Ipswich

Monster

M y monster is Mister Moody
O range fur
Ofte **N** sits on the couch
S mart and spiky
T iny and ticklish
E ats candyfloss with sprinkles on top
R est and running.

Marcello Moore (7)
Morland Primary School, Ipswich

Monster

M y monster is moody.
O ften quiet and silly.
N aughty and noisy.
S neaky and silly.
T wenty hairs and spiky horns.
E ats rotten eggs.
R otten teeth and ears.

Harry Upson (6)
Morland Primary School, Ipswich

Monster

M y monster is stinky.
O nly my monster has makeup on.
N eeds to eat kids.
S tomps in tunnels.
T icklish monster.
E ats lots of junk.
R eally sharp nails.

Angelica Porter (7)
Morland Primary School, Ipswich

Charlotte

C ute monster
H uge spikes
A ngry mouth
R ude monster
L ong hair
O range fur
T errifying teeth
T eary monster
E xciting spikes.

Skyla Clark (6)
Morland Primary School, Ipswich

Monster

M akes horrible slime.
O range fur that is slimy.
N eeds a bath.
S leeps in the morning.
T ries to steal children.
E yes are red.
R uns really quick.

Lucia Jordan (7)
Morland Primary School, Ipswich

Monster

M y monster is silly.
O range and slimy.
N eeds to brush.
S cary and slimy.
T ough and also fights.
E ats slime, also grows food.
R uns really fast.

Zamar Oduro Bonsu (7)
Morland Primary School, Ipswich

Monster

M y monster is mean
O range, fluffy fur
N aughty
S mall and silly
T icklish and like a teddy bear
E ating eyes, kids and heads
R oaring really loud.

Abigail Javier (7)
Morland Primary School, Ipswich

Monster

M ean and grumpy.
O ne googly eye.
N eeds a bath.
S harp, smelly teeth.
T oes tickle children.
E ats rotten onions.
R eally poor.

Freyah Baker (6)
Morland Primary School, Ipswich

Monster

M akes gooey slime
O nly eats gross rubbish
N aughty and scary
S cary and scary
T wenty eyes
E xtra mouth
R uns really fast.

Santhosh Ramkumar (7)
Morland Primary School, Ipswich

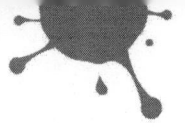

Monster

M ean monster
O range eyes
N ame is Marshall
S porty monster
T all monster
E gg-shaped head
R ocket booster feet and hands.

Leo Marshall (7)
Morland Primary School, Ipswich

Shaun

S illy and slimy, it's simmy!
H appy and hairy and big
A ggressive, angry, 'appy
U pset sometimes because no friends!
N ice and naughty.

Ashlee Kerry (6)
Morland Primary School, Ipswich

Monster

M ean and naughty
O ften gets players
N oisy players
S laps drowsy players
T ongue is very wet
E ats rubbish
R uns fast.

Max Hill (6)
Morland Primary School, Ipswich

Monster

M y monster is funny and crazy
O ften silly
N oisy and happy
S mall and slimy
T wo years old
E ats bugs
R eally fast.

Amila Notkute (6)
Morland Primary School, Ipswich

Monster

M ean and mad
O ften eats animals
N aughty and nosy
S o he sucks blood
T ummy is electric
E ats people
R otten egg.

Joey Bantoft (7)
Morland Primary School, Ipswich

The Monster Is Scary

M onster is scary
O range legs
N oisy stomps
S limy skin
T eeth are scary
E ats rotten eggs
R oars loudly.

Harley Carden (7)
Morland Primary School, Ipswich

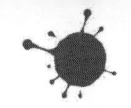

Monster

M ean and evil
O range fur
N ibbles flowers
S limy monster
T ickles children
E ats leaves
R uns fast.

Kasia Borowicka (7)
Morland Primary School, Ipswich

Monster

M ean and grumpy
O ne googly eye
N aughty
S cary
T eeth are sharp
E ats children
R uns fast.

Sam Tunner (7)
Morland Primary School, Ipswich

Splat

S plat is very long.
P eas are Splat's favourite.
L ittle bouncy ball.
A nts are his friends.
T errible toes.

Logan Pennock (4)
Morland Primary School, Ipswich

Splat

S plat is a monster
P asta is my favourite
L oves to eat sausages
A nts are my friends
T iny ears and toes.

Rogan Sesto (5)
Morland Primary School, Ipswich

Splat

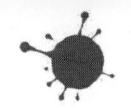

S plat is orange
P eople love him
L isten to him laugh
A nts are his friends
T errible ears and toes.

Harry Norman (5)
Morland Primary School, Ipswich

Splat

S plat is a monster
P asta is my favourite
L oves pineapple
A nts are my friends
T eeth are huge.

Cavalli-Lee Waight (4)
Morland Primary School, Ipswich

Splat

S plat is orange
P eople love him
L isten to him laugh
A nts are his friends
T iny ears and toes.

Dulcie Rouse (5)
Morland Primary School, Ipswich

Millie

M any eyes
I nteresting arms
L ong legs
L ong arms
I nteresting legs
E xciting face.

Lola Wintrup (6)
Morland Primary School, Ipswich

Godsila

G ood monster
O ne yellow eye
D izzy
S illy
I ll
L ong arms
A big body.

Jax Pretlove (6)
Morland Primary School, Ipswich

Splat

S plat is a monster
P eople love him
L oves to eat pizza
A nts are my friends
T errible eyes.

Scarlett Lewis (4)
Morland Primary School, Ipswich

Splat

S plat has rocket feet
P ink, spiky fingers
L ittle grey legs
A rms are long
T errible teeth.

Riley Davis (5)
Morland Primary School, Ipswich

Daisy

D irty monster
A nnoying monster
I ncredible eyes monster
S limy skin monster
Y ucky monster.

Rosie Minns (5)
Morland Primary School, Ipswich

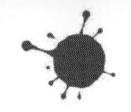

My Monster Wobbly

M enacing
O ne eye
N ice
S illy
T errifying
E xcitable
R eally purple.

Sienna Worby (4)
Morland Primary School, Ipswich

My Monster Crazy

M enacing
O dd
N eat
S cary
T all
E xcitable
R eally, terribly crazy.

Maxwell Ologunja (5)
Morland Primary School, Ipswich

Splat

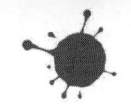

S plat is a monster
P eople love him
L oves bananas
A nts are his friends
T errible mouth.

Sienna Bantoft (4)
Morland Primary School, Ipswich

Creepy

C reeps
R ed
E xtra big eyes
E xcellent brain
P erfect monster
Y ellow tongue.

Conor Mortimer (5)
Morland Primary School, Ipswich

Splat

S plat is a monster
P eople love him
L oves noodles
A nts are his friends
T errible toes.

Ovidas Cizas (5)
Morland Primary School, Ipswich

Smiley

S illy
M unches grass
I nteresting
L ong ears
E yes are green
Y ellow boots.

Scarlett Chapman (5)
Morland Primary School, Ipswich

My Monster Yahavee

M enacing
O ne eye
N eat
S pecial
T errifying
E xcitable
R ound.

Tabitha Robinson Kathirchelvan (5)
Morland Primary School, Ipswich

My Monster Marv

- **M** ulticoloured
- **O** ld
- **N** eat
- **S** mall
- **T** all
- **E** normous
- **R** eally hairy.

Kayden Kalyia (5)
Morland Primary School, Ipswich

My Monster Emily

M ulticoloured
O dd
N eat
S illy
T all
E normous
R eally hairy.

Kinsley Broadhurst (5)
Morland Primary School, Ipswich

My Monster Hairy

M iniature
O dd
N ice
S pecial
T iny
E xcitable
R eally hairy.

Archie Pike (4)
Morland Primary School, Ipswich

Mini

M ini is a purple monster
I ncredible, hairy monster
N aughty, big monster
I nside a huge cage.

Mya Broadhurst (6)
Morland Primary School, Ipswich

My Monster Logan

M enacing
O dd
N eat
S illy
T errifying
E vil
R eally crazy.

Marley Wells (5)
Morland Primary School, Ipswich

My Monster Flower

M enacing
O dd
N eat
S illy
T errifying
E vil
R eally crazy.

Sofia Theobald (4)
Morland Primary School, Ipswich

My Monster Unicorn

M enacing
O dd
N ice
S illy
T all
E xcitable
R eally smiley.

Peyton Garner (5)
Morland Primary School, Ipswich

My Monster Colourfy

M enacing
O ld
N eat
S illy
T all
E xcitable
R ed and blue.

Edena Brazlauskaite (5)
Morland Primary School, Ipswich

Slime

S melly and slimy
L ong, sharp teeth
I t smells bad
M ucky monster
E eny nose.

Amelia Baker (5)
Morland Primary School, Ipswich

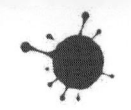

Celeo

C aring
E ats candy
L ikes to explore
E nergetic
O verexcited very easily.

Luna Usman (6)
Morland Primary School, Ipswich

My Monster Hairy

M enacing
O ld
N eat
S miley
T all
E xcitable
R ed.

Olivia Garwood (4)
Morland Primary School, Ipswich

My Monster Arthur

M ean
O dd
N eat
S illy
T errifying
E vil
R ough.

Arthur Davies (5)
Morland Primary School, Ipswich

My Monster Holly

M enacing
O ld
N eat
S cary
T all
E vil
R ed.

Riley Richmond (5)
Morland Primary School, Ipswich

My Monster Scary

M ean
O ld
N eat
S miley
T iny
E vil
R ed.

Remy Hunt (5)
Morland Primary School, Ipswich

Jimmy

J ust slimy
I nteresting
M unchy
M oany
Y ellow fur.

Hunter Drury (5)
Morland Primary School, Ipswich

Mila

M y monster is big.
I t sinks.
L ots of spikes.
A lot of fur.

Oliver Baldry (6)
Morland Primary School, Ipswich

Zeus

Z eus eats teachers
E xciting
U ses his laser eyes
S uperhero.

Leo Kelly (6)
Morland Primary School, Ipswich

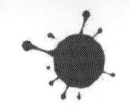

Sniff

S appy
N aughty
I mpressive
F urry
F luffy.

Piper Simpson (6)
Morland Primary School, Ipswich

Pond

P olite
O range skin
N ice eyes
D reams about spiders.

Hazel Garnham (6)
Morland Primary School, Ipswich

Mila

M ini monster.
I s scary.
L onely.
A happy monster.

Karson Thompson (6)
Morland Primary School, Ipswich

Obyg

O range spots
B ig
Y ucky
G reen.

Arthur Heasman (6)
Morland Primary School, Ipswich

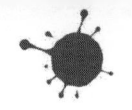

Fast

F at
A ngry
S cary
T all.

Oscar Holder (6)
Morland Primary School, Ipswich

Be As Evil As A Monster

C oming near, watch
O ut! He's here.
S ounds like thunder.
T errible attitude!
O n the
M ountain shooting
F ire out of his hands.
I ts angriness scares everybody.
R oars and roars!
M outh chomps like a lion. He's
U gly and
E vil.

Mirabel Anyanwu (6)
New Silksworth Academy, New Silksworth

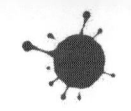

Fireball

F iery eye
I n its hand, there is fire
R isks people's lives
E vil thinking
B right wings
A mazing fire tricks
L oves fire
L ook out!

Alana Mullins (6)
New Silksworth Academy, New Silksworth

Monster Bob

O ogly smile
S melly breath
C atches diseases
A lways angry
R eady to gobble you up.

B ig head
O range tummy
B etter watch out!

Reuben Frame (6)
New Silksworth Academy, New Silksworth

Stinkybob!

S nots
T oenails
I tchy legs
N aughty monster
K nobbly knees
Y ucky
B lobby hands
O ne eye
B ig Stinkybob!

Scarlett Bird (6)
New Silksworth Academy, New Silksworth

Limee

L ikes to play in sand
I t likes to play with me
M ay eat slime sometimes
E veryone thinks he's friendly and he is
E njoys watching TV.

Michelle Anyanwu (6)
New Silksworth Academy, New Silksworth

My Teddy

F ire
I cky sticky
R avenous
E vil eye
B arbed
A lien
L ight green
L oveable Teddy.

Louisa Davidson (5)
New Silksworth Academy, New Silksworth

Zippy

Z ips around the park
I t's crazy
P inging at the arcades
P laying tag
Y awning when he's tired.

CharlieAnn Docherty (6)
New Silksworth Academy, New Silksworth

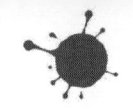

Blue Gas

B lue as a shooting star.
L uminous as a lovely sunset.
U seful as a volcano explosion.
E nding of a shooting star.

G liding through all of London.
A nd the Antarctic also.
S outh America and North America.

Bailey Jones (7)
St Philip's CE Primary School, Salford

Pinky

P inky likes to rob some money
I nstead of eating slime, Pinky eats money
N ow it is time to eat some pink slimy slime
K ind monster gives giant, pink, slimy, sprinkling slime
Y ou are a giant, yellow, sparkling, slimy monster.

Cheryl Chick (7)
St Philip's CE Primary School, Salford

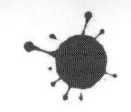

Spidy

S neaks on precious and juicy prey.
P repare for a gloomy, miserable death.
I nspired by organised, mean monsters.
D angerous, mean and scary cobwebs.
Y ears and years, nobody has been to the flexible, bloody spider.

Aydin Tumusime (6)
St Philip's CE Primary School, Salford

Ronauld

R onauld is as tall as a skyscraper.
O rganised as a mum.
N ightmarish as living with werewolves.
A t the cinema.
U rgent as a mission.
L aser eyes.
D aring as a survivor.

George Burton (7)
St Philip's CE Primary School, Salford

Hydra

H ydra is as hideous as a tiger.
Y ucky as a rotten, expired egg.
D emon if you're awake at night.
R ampaging through the town like a devil.
A nightmare like a living werewolf.

Liam Nduonofit (7)
St Philip's CE Primary School, Salford

Spark

S park likes to eat flaming hot fire.
P ranking kids with amazing, brilliant jokes.
A s boiling as a kettle burning.
R oars as loud as a lion.
K eeps pushing like a bowling ball.

Albie Thorpe (7)
St Philip's CE Primary School, Salford

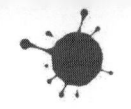

Sofia

S ofia is a pretty monster creeping and crawling
O h, I wish I was in the sky
F irst I stalk people and then I eat them
I 'll be supportive of my friends
A lways in the sky.

Elaine Ibrahim (6)
St Philip's CE Primary School, Salford

Fire

F ire is horrifying, creepy and miniature.
I nstead of chicken, he eats slimy slime.
R obbing the gigantic bank, shop and the factory.
E xcited for shiny red, blue and green slime.

Jimmi Cheung (7)
St Philip's CE Primary School, Salford

Blad

B eady eye for delicious prey.
L ight tail for moving its tail.
A greedy monster devouring his prey.
D evilish monster devouring his prey.

Sean Tsang (7)
St Philip's CE Primary School, Salford

Luna

L una is as beautiful as flowers.
U sually good but sometimes bad.
N ot helpful that much.
A lways nice, kind and sometimes helpful.

Hollie Wraight (7)
St Philip's CE Primary School, Salford

Senin

S cruffy as an eagle.
E nergy for exercise.
N ibbles smooth fingers.
I ncredible eyes.
N utrition from delicious pizza.

Christopher Kwok (6)
St Philip's CE Primary School, Salford

Firey

F irey has a burnt body.
I nteresting, jagged horns.
R eally colourful body.
E nergetic legs.
Y ummy, cheesy burgers.

Victoria Lyu (6)
St Philip's CE Primary School, Salford

Star

S cary as a slimy lizard.
T earing paper like a tiger.
A gloomy eye for seeing in the dark.
R eally dull and luminous skin.

Harriett Paisley (7)
St Philip's CE Primary School, Salford

Lil

L oves eating juicy strawberry slime.
I ce is cold for her because it's in the fridge.
L oves playing hide-and-seek.

Leena Tijani (7)
St Philip's CE Primary School, Salford

Sai

S luggy as a slimy snail
A s horrible as a skeleton
I s as evil as an unkind demon.

Othman Aljasim (8)
St Philip's CE Primary School, Salford

Friendly

F ally is my monster friend and she loves being happy but one thing, people think she's scary
R eally helpful and her fluff is pink
I nside her feelings are love and she loves ice cream
E xcited for school, she loves it
N osy sometimes
D rawing a picture is our favourite thing
L oud as a monster friend
Y esterday we went to the park and she loved it.

Izabella Sharp (7)
Ysgol Bryn Garth Primary School, Penyffordd

Adorable

A t four in the morning, she plays in the garden
D on't be scared, she doesn't roar or bite
O nly drawing and playing
R eally she is just a blob
A really small blob!
B lobs is her name by the way
L ittle Blobs sleeps by your window at night
E ven in the dark.

Natalie Talay-Lopez (6)
Ysgol Bryn Garth Primary School, Penyffordd

Mr Gredy

M r Gredy is his name
R ice is my monster's favourite food.

G ood monster because nobody loved him
R eally sad is my monster
E ight arms like an octopus
D on't feed him too much 'cause he goes crazy
Y ou, Mr Gredy! Will you be my friend?

Lewis Lacey (7)
Ysgol Bryn Garth Primary School, Penyffordd

Blobby

- **B** est monster because he's funny
- **L** et me tell you my monster's name, Blobby
- **O** ctopus legs, he has four tentacle legs
- **B** ossiest monster in the world
- **B** usy monster all the time
- **Y** ellow ears that can hear well.

Ivy Johns (6)
Ysgol Bryn Garth Primary School, Penyffordd

Floppy

F abulous horns on top of his head
L uscious green fur
O ctober's his birthday
P eople play with him all the time
P olice say he is wonderful
Y ou've got to watch out when Floppy is about.

Willow Peyton (7)
Ysgol Bryn Garth Primary School, Penyffordd

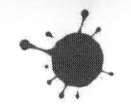

Spike

S ome people are scared of Spike.
P eople think he is a dab monster.
I like him because he is kind.
K ind and thoughtful, he loves me and I love him.
E veryone should have a monster like him.

Hallie Jones (7)
Ysgol Bryn Garth Primary School, Penyffordd

Nervous

N obody likes her
E lla is my monster's name
R eally scary
V ery old
O nly chases little people
U nder the bed, she sleeps
S he is hungry all the time.

Heidi Jones (6)
Ysgol Bryn Garth Primary School, Penyffordd

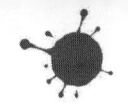

Angry

A ndrew is my monster's name.
N obody knows he loves football.
G oalkeeping record breaker.
R unning fast, he won the race.
Y ay! He got ice cream.

Lottie Tellett Danks (7)
Ysgol Bryn Garth Primary School, Penyffordd

Hairy

H airy McLere is my monster's name.
A nger makes him explode into fire.
I f he can see you, he will chase you.
R un away!
Y ou will get bitten!

Louie Farbrace-Bellis (7)
Ysgol Bryn Garth Primary School, Penyffordd

Dark

D ark is my friend, I feed her fish
A little mouse became friends with Dark
R uns as fast as a cheetah
K ind as can be, I love her.

Esme Roberts (7)
Ysgol Bryn Garth Primary School, Penyffordd

Fierce

F un and scary
I t chases dogs
E ats people
R ides a bike
C an be fiery
E very day.

Niamh Power (5)
Ysgol Bryn Garth Primary School, Penyffordd

Greedy

G reat games
R eally hungry
E normous
E vil sometimes
D eadly
Y ells a lot.

Margo Johns (6)
Ysgol Bryn Garth Primary School, Penyffordd

Smelly

S neaky
M onstrous
E vil
L oud
L azy
Y ellow.

Charlie Palmer (5)
Ysgol Bryn Garth Primary School, Penyffordd

Scary

S uper mad
C razy
A ngry
R ound
Y ells really loud.

Zed Galing (6)
Ysgol Bryn Garth Primary School, Penyffordd

Stomp

- **S** mart
- **T** all
- **O** range and pink
- **M** agic
- **P** retty.

Eliza Lavelle (5)
Ysgol Bryn Garth Primary School, Penyffordd

Slimy

S cary
L oud
I nteresting
M ad
Y ells a lot.

Layla Lister (6)
Ysgol Bryn Garth Primary School, Penyffordd

Scary

S limy
C hases you
A fraid
R ich
Y ucky.

Faith Jones (7)
Ysgol Bryn Garth Primary School, Penyffordd

Young Writers
Est. 1991

Young Writers Information

We hope you have enjoyed reading this book – and that you will continue to in the coming years.

If you're the parent or family member of an enthusiastic poet or story writer, do visit our website **www.youngwriters.co.uk/subscribe** and sign up to receive news, competitions, writing challenges and tips, activities and much, much more! There's lots to keep budding writers motivated!

If you would like to order further copies of this book, or any of our other titles, then please give us a call or order via your online account.

Young Writers
Remus House
Coltsfoot Drive
Peterborough
PE2 9BF
(01733) 890066
info@youngwriters.co.uk

Join in the conversation!
Tips, news, giveaways and much more!

f YoungWritersUK   **✕** YoungWritersCW   **◎** youngwriterscw

Scan me to watch the
Monster Acrostics Video